MW00677756

Treasures of the Heart

of the

Donna Christopher

ISBN 978-1-64468-478-8 (Paperback)
ISBN 978-1-64468-479-5 (Hardcover)
ISBN 978-1-64468-480-1 (Digital)

Copyright © 2020 Donna Christopher
All rights reserved
First Edition

All rights reserved. No part of this publication may be reproduced, distributed, or transmitted in any form or by any means, including photocopying, recording, or other electronic or mechanical methods without the prior written permission of the publisher. For permission requests, solicit the publisher via the address below.

Covenant Books, Inc.
11661 Hwy 707
Murrells Inlet, SC 29576
www.covenantbooks.com

Dedicated to my mother, Willie Mae Smith.

A collection of short stories and poems of times,
When Jesus was real in our lives.
These are treasures of my heart.

A special thank you to my dearest friends.
I would not have completed this book without you.

Photography by Candace Swing and myself.

I hope you enjoy the treasures of my heart.

Chapter 1

Christmas of Perfect Love

Christmas

Can I read you a Christmas Story, my love?
One that will calm your spirit and give you peace;
Can I sit by your side and read you
The Christmas Story my dear?
One that will put a gentle smile on your face
And help you sleep tonight;
Can I lay next to you and read you
This Christmas Story, my child?
One that will wipe away all your tears
And let you know someone who loves you is very near;
Can I look into your face as I read you
This Christmas Story, my friend?
One that was written long ago
And is the greatest story ever told;
Can I read to you what Christmas really is my love?
It begins with a gift from above given to mankind as perfect love…

Christmas begins with Christ.

It's a Christmas Event

And so it was, that, while they were there, the days were accomplished that she should be delivered.

And she brought forth her firstborn son, and wrapped him in swaddling clothes, and laid him in a manger; because there was no room for them in the inn.

And there were in the same country shepherds abiding in the field, keeping watch over their flock by night.

And, lo, the angel of the Lord came upon them, and the glory of the Lord shone round about them: and they were sore afraid.

And the angel said unto them, Fear not: for, behold, I bring you good tidings of great joy, which shall be to all people.

For unto you is born this day in the city of David a Savior, which is Christ the Lord.

And this shall be a sign unto you; Ye shall find the babe wrapped in swaddling clothes, lying in a manger.

And suddenly there was with the angel a multitude of the heavenly host praising God, and saying,

Glory to God in the highest, and on earth peace, good will toward men. (Luke 2:6–14)

A Christmas of perfect love.

Christmas Memory

The church sanctuary is decorated with green trees and garland, red ribbons and berries, and white tree lights against the white walls. It is such a beautiful sight this Sunday morning.

The choir before us stands and sings Christmas carols. The people in the congregation sing a couple with them. When they are finished, they come down and sit with the rest of the congregation. There is a special love and peace among the people this particular morning.

The pastor steps up to the pulpit. At that moment, I sense a change in things. What was beautiful becomes more beautiful.

The pastor has his red jacket on with a red tie and black pants. He starts to speak. He begins to tell us about Jesus. Over and over, he speaks of only Jesus. He sings at different times. He continues to preach and then he cries. He sings again and cries again.

I begin thinking, this is a gift from Jesus. He is giving us a special gift. As our pastor weeps, it is such a humbling sight. The Lord is letting us see him, touching our pastor.

The people in the congregation began to weep. I weep as well as the Holy Spirit touches our hearts too. The Lord has visited with us this Christmas morning.

Happy Birthday, Jesus.
We love you.

In a Small Country Town

Around eight o'clock on Christmas Eve morning, we arrived to work on time. This will be a short workday in reverence to Christmas, Jesus's birthday. We opened the lobby with the Christmas trees decorated and the Christmas lights on. The light from the fireplace burned warmly in the sitting area. I can see it burning from where I work. It is so beautiful.

Customers start coming in, one or two at a time, to take care of their business. They continued to stream in and out all during the morning and afternoon. I talked with several of them. Some were happy and smiling, and some had that special look on their faces that you only see at Christmas time. I asked them if they were ready for Christmas, and they said yes because it was here! Some people were not happy at all. Some said they would be glad when it was over. Some just shook their heads not wanting any part of it.

Another one of our customers, who is a singer, came in with his guitar. He was so happy and had a beautiful smile on his face. He said he was at home and thought, *I am supposed to be somewhere today.* He looked over at his guitar leaning against the wall. He reached for it and came to see us. This customer started walking around while playing and singing Christmas songs for everyone in the lobby.

People were watching and listening while taking care of their business and talking with each other. There were lots of cheerful chatter going on in the lobby now. Then someone asked him to sing Silent Night. He started singing. As he sang about our Savior's birth, the whole lobby grew silent. No one spoke a word, and no one made a sound. Peace filled the room.

As he continued to sing, I felt Jesus so strongly that it was all I could do to continue with my work. These different kinds of people with different kinds of lives and problems were listening to this song.

> Silent night, holy night! All is calm,
> all is bright
> Round yon Virgin, Mother and Child
> Holy Infant so Tender and mild,
> Sleep in heavenly peace,
> Sleep in heavenly peace,
> Silent night, holy night!
> Shepherds quake at the sight!
> Glories stream from heaven afar,
> Heavenly hosts sing
> Al-le-lu-ia!
> Christ the Savior is born!
> Christ the Savior is born!

I honestly can't tell you how many verses he sang, but I can tell you Jesus knew what was going on because hearts were being touched with the message of the Savior's birth.

> And she brought forth her firstborn son, and
> wrapped him in swaddling clothes, and laid him
> in a manger, because there was no room for them
> in the inn. And there were in the same country
> shepherds abiding in the field, keeping watch
> over their flock by night. And, lo, the angel of
> the Lord came upon them, and the glory of the
> Lord shone round about them: and they were
> sore afraid. And the angel said unto them, Fear
> not: for, behold, I bring you good tidings of great
> joy, which shall be **to all people**. For unto you
> is born this day in the city of David a Saviour,
> which is Christ the Lord. And this shall be a
> sign unto you; Ye shall find the babe wrapped in

swaddling clothes, lying in a manger. And suddenly there was with the angel a multitude of the heavenly host praising God, and saying, Glory to God in the highest and on earth peace, good will toward men. (Luke 2:7–14)

Merry Christmas!

Home for Christmas

It was the Sunday before Christmas in 2015. The church parking lot was filled with cars as we arrived for Sunday school this morning. Couples were walking closely together through the parking area as they made their way to the front door.

Entering the foyer to the right is a nativity scene for all to see. Men in their black suits and red ties were gathered together, smiling and greeting everyone as they walked through the foyer.

As we entered the sanctuary and look down the aisle, we see decorations of green garland and wreaths with red and silver ribbons and little white lights. They are so pretty against the white walls of the sanctuary.

The green Christmas trees with white lights are located on each corner of the choir loft. Red poinsettias are situated across the front and around the altar. On the seat of each pew lay unopened envelopes, waiting to be opened by the people who normally sit there.

We continue to walk down the aisle and sliding along the pew to our usual places as we've done many times before. A sweet friend came in and sat down beside me. The unopened envelopes lay along our pew. We gathered together—the ones addressed to each of us and our families. My friend had his envelopes in his hand and mine were in my lap. He started opening his, and I did as well. We opened one at a time and read it. Each one was a beautiful Christmas Card. We showed each other the pictures on front of our cards, but kept the names on the inside, to ourselves. Each name on the inside warmed our hearts as we read them.

As we continued to read our cards, the pastor walked up and shook our hand and said hello. No matter what we had been through, nor the different places and celebrations we have had this Christmas, being here this morning feels like coming home for Christmas.

The warmth, love, peace, complete acceptance, and loving chatter filled the sanctuary as we continued reading and sharing our Christmas cards that was left for each of us. God is so good.

After Sunday school, the choir and music minister were ready to sing. Some of the choir members wore red, and the faces of each person were smiling and glowing.

As we watched the choir and our pastor in front of the decorations, I was thinking, I wish we had a picture of this. It would make a beautiful Christmas card to give our family and friends. As they sang, the music was so beautiful that it made me cry. It was like a healing ointment soothing my soul. When the choir finished singing, they came down to have a seat among the rest of us.

The pastor was at the pulpit now. The church was full. There didn't seem to be any room left for anyone else to sit.

The pastor told us about worshipping Jesus, about Christ's birth and who he was born for. He said that Jesus was born and died for all. To the great and the lowly, to the wicked and the holy, he came for everyone.

No matter who you are or what you do or where you came from, he came for you. He did it all for you. Why don't you come to Jesus, he is waiting.

When the pastor finished, the people went to the altar to pray. Jesus met them there.

It was good to come home for Christmas with family, friends and Jesus!

He came to me, when I could not come to where he was, he came to me.
Nothing gives the believer so much joy as fellowship with Christ.

Mama's Christmas Memory

While talking with Mama this week, she told me of a Christmas long ago. Mama had six children, three boys and three girls. One of the girls went to heaven when she was a child. This broke her heart and would be something she would never be able to overcome. But Jesus stayed close to her heart through all the years to come.

When her children became adults, their lives took them in different directions, making them unable to come home for Christmas, all at the same time.

Except for this one particular Christmas, everyone came home on Christmas Day. Mom said that night she went to bed and talked to Jesus for a while. Now years later, she remembers praying, "Lord I saw them all today, all but one." Then she fell asleep.

Later that night, she awoke and sat straight up in the bed. Her voice began to quiver as she described in detail what she had seen.

She saw a large field of green clover. On the other side of the field, she saw a red-haired little girl, running through the clover toward her.

Then she laid back down. Before she went to sleep, she prayed, "Thank you, Lord, I saw them all today."

The Lord is close to the broken hearted.
Remember the treasure and what the Lord has done
for you. Then tell someone what he has done.

Christmas 2019

It was one Sunday morning in December when Jim and I had gone to church together. Upon arrival at the church, we found the parking lot completely filled with all kinds of vehicles. However, we did find a place to park on the grassy area and made our way to the front door of the church. When we entered the church, the foyer was decorated so beautifully that I seemed to have forgotten Jim was with me.

Both sides of the foyer were decorated with nativity scenes. I walked slowly to the door of the sanctuary, not wanting to miss one tiny detail. This was more than mere decorations. It was being in Church, seeing and experiencing all the things about Jesus.

We entered the sanctuary. Love and joy shown on every face we see. God's people are so beautiful this morning. We sat down in our usual places. The sanctuary was decorated with Christmas wreaths and green garland and Christmas trees. Each one has white Christmas lights on them. I sat quietly while taking it all in.

The people in the choir were getting ready to sing. Our music minister led us in song. The music and songs were all about Jesus and seamed to go straight into my heart. Then we felt the presence of the true and living God. Oh, how I love this place. I can't tell you much about what happened after that. Only that it was an awesome song service.

Then our pastor stepped up to the pulpit. He began to sing:

"Down From His Glory"
O how I love him!
How I adore him!
My breath, my sunshine, and my all in all.

The great Creator became my Savior, and
all God's fullness dwelleth in him.

He began to deliver the sermon. It felt like he is preaching to only me, and again, it went straight into my heart. He said God is in control and that it's in the Savior's hands. He said it several times. Tears streamed down my face, but I wasn't crying. He preached so much more than can be told.

I am so thankful for these people and this church. But most of all, I'm thankful for Jesus saving me. This is what he came down from his glory to do.

Merry Christmas

Only a person who knows Jesus understands
what Christmas is all about.
Want you accept this priceless gift of salvation today?

The Christmas Tree

I met a man today and asked him if he was ready for Christmas. His reply was not what one would expect. He said that with all the hardships, family problems, and hurts, Christmas didn't mean so much. When he finished talking, Jesus started bringing a memory to my mind. Before realizing what was happening, I had begun telling this man about it.

I started with explaining how sometimes Jesus will touch your heart when you least expect it and how he had touched mine just a couple of days before.

It was one dark and foggy evening while driving home when it became very difficult to see the road. The darkness and fog were so thick it seemed to cover the whole world. There weren't any car lights or people anywhere to be seen. Just total darkness in every direction.

Then finally, arriving at a red light, glowing in the darkness and fog, at the intersection of Hwy 400 and Burnt Stand Road, I was relieved that it would not be much further before arriving home. I sat there in the darkness, gazing over at the car lot located on the corner of the intersection.

The people at the car lot had made a huge Christmas tree out of white Christmas lights. It seemed to be taller than the power poles. In complete darkness and fog, the white lights of the Christmas tree glowed luminously.

While waiting there and looking at the tree, the Lord touched my heart. The lights of the Christmas tree glowing in the darkness and fog reminded me of the birth of our Savior.

Then the same man began sharing with me about a small town he had visited and how beautiful it was being decorated with Christmas lights and how it touched his heart being there and seeing it. He finished by saying that we need to be sensitive to Jesus's touch. Then our conversation was over, and the man had to leave.

I think we both know now, even though there may not be enough money to buy the things you want or maybe your heart has been broken so badly that you can't feel, Jesus's love will shine through to your heart.

While you are looking at the Christmas decorations this year, let it remind you of Jesus's birthday, and there is someone who knows what you are going through, and he loves you.

> Then spake Jesus again unto them, saying, I am the
> light of the world: he that followeth me shall not
> walk in darkness, but shall have the light of life.
> —John 8:12

This world is dark as midnight, Jesus has come that by faith we may have light and may no longer sit in the gloom which covers all the rest of mankind.

Darkness makes the light of holiness and righteousness of God brighter.

Hummingbirds and Sparrows

It was a cold winter morning, while looking out the window, when I saw a tiny hummingbird. He was all alone at the bird feeder trying to get a drink.

Knowing the nectar must be frozen. I went out to get the feeder, brought it inside, and sat it in front of a warming vent. When the nectar became warm, I carried it back out in hopes of helping the little bird.

The little bird stayed there, drinking the warm nectar with his feathers all fluffed up, which makes him look much larger than he really is. I wondered how this tiny bird could survive such cold weather.

Sometimes, a hummingbird will fly into the garage then not being able to find his way out, will become trapped.

The garage is attached to the house with windows on one side. The entrance to the garage remains open without any doors.

When the hummingbird flies into the garage, he goes to the window and tries to get out. He will try over and over to fly through the window until he wears himself down.

At that point, I can go over and catch him in my hands and gently carry him to the opening of the garage and set him free. Then the hummingbird flies away.

With a little research on hummingbirds and sparrows, I discovered how special their bodies were made and what kind of food they require to survive. It is quite amazing how God takes care of every tiny detail that concerns them.

The sparrows and hummingbirds remind me of how much Jesus loves us and how he knows every detail concerning us.

He knows every time we get worn down from trying. Then He holds us so gently in his hands and takes us through each trying time.

This Christmas, while you are celebrating the birth of our Lord and Savior Jesus Christ, just know even though his eye is on the sparrow, you are of more value than many sparrows to Him.

And she brought forth her firstborn son,
and wrapped him in swaddling clothes, and
laid him in a manger; because there was no
room for them in the inn. (Luke 2:7)
For unto you is born this day in the
city of David a Saviour, which is
Christ the Lord. (Luke 2:11)

Merry Christmas

*I sing because I'm happy, I sing because I'm free.
His eye is on the sparrow, and I know he watches me.*

Oh Come Let Us Adore Him

Oh Lord my Savior, I adore you. It is Christmas time, and I want to write a feel-good Christmas story, but all I see is pain, hurt, and struggle.

Someone's child has passed away. A friend is so sick. Other children are having problems. People can't afford to buy the food they need or the things to take care of their self and their loved ones while some people are oblivious to these great needs.

Then for a moment, fear runs through me because losing a child is the greatest pain I can imagine. How do we carry on? How do we have enough strength to make another day after experiencing or knowing and seeing all these things happening?

Then I remember you and what you did. How you saved my soul and came into my heart and life. I remember where you came from and what you went through for an old sinner like me. Then I feel your presence. It is you and your grace that helps us through these devastating times. When all we want to do is scream, *why?*

Now my soul sings:
O come all ye faithful, Joyful and triumphant,
O come ye, O come ye to Bethlehem,
Come and behold Him, Born the King of angles,
O come let us adore Him, O come let us adore
Him, O come let us adore Him
Christ the Lord

Little Dove

As I lay down to sleep tonight, the thoughts of a baby girl at church and my little granddaughter run through my mind. It was such a blessing being with them in church this morning.

The baby and her family sat in front of my family. When the congregation stood to sing, the baby wanted me to hold her and began climbing up her mommy. So, I reached down and pulled her up into my arms. Her mommy, whose name is Dove, and her husband, looked at me with disbelief. They said she never goes to anyone. But Little Dove came to me the best way she could.

As I pulled Little Dove up to my chest, she lay her head on my shoulder. I felt her arms go around me as far as they could, and her legs stretched around my waist. We stood there together for a few moments. It was so awesome.

The congregation sat down, my granddaughter Pennie, sat on one side of me and Jim on the other side. But Little Dove sat on my lap. She was so happy and at peace. I was a total stranger to her, and she wanted to be with me.

While thinking about Little Dove and what she did, the thoughts of Jesus and Zacchaeus came to mind. How Zacchaeus climbed up the sycamore tree, just to see Jesus pass by and how Jesus stopped and spoke to Zacchaeus. While thinking about them I realized we should do everything we can to come to Jesus, to be in His presence, lay our head on His shoulder and trust that He will take care of us no matter what comes our way…

Merry Christmas
2019

The Voice of Tears

It was early New Year's Eve morning 2019 when my five-year-old granddaughter and three-year-old grandson, whose names are Pennie and Wyatt, came over to spend the day.

Upon their arrival I noticed Pennie laid down on the recliner, which is not like her. I walked over and sat down beside her and began to rub her head.

She looked up and said my tummy hurts. At that moment a sense of urgency ran through me. I needed to move fast.

I ran and grabbed a garbage pail and wash cloths. When I returned, she sat up and said, oh my tummy hurts and started throwing up.

This little girl continued throwing up every 3 to 5 minutes intervals. I washed her face each time, then she would throw up again. It would not stop. I gave her sips of water; she would throw up. Then sips of Gatorade, she threw that up.

I text her mommy, she is trying to get off work to come take care of her little girl. She is still throwing up.

I sit down on the floor at her feet and hold her feet in my hands. While rubbing and caressing them, I lay my face on them and kiss them. She is so sick.

While her feet are in my hands and my face on her feet, I begin to cry. That is when Jesus heard the voice of tears and touched little Pennie. The crying becomes so strong I need to leave the room. When I return she is sitting there smiling at me.

No more tummy hurting nor throwing up. Mommy doesn't need to come home now.

Pennie is ready to have breakfast.

She sits at the table and smiles at me again. We both know what has happened.

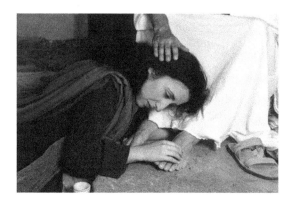

"Jesus hears the voice of our tears"

Chapter 2

Faith, Hope, and Love

While Living in a Troubled World

Sunday mornings in our church create sweet memories that linger throughout the day and the week ahead. From the drive to church, going into the sanctuary and gathering together for Sunday school, to the Sunday morning worship service, there is something special about each one. The sweet spirit that fills this place and on each person's face that I meet lets me know I am where I'm supposed to be.

For Sunday school, we gather together with our own age groups. We share with the class what we have on our hearts that needs prayer. Then we pray for all the requests. Next, our teacher teaches us from the pages of the King James Bible.

An hour later, the worship service begins. The music minister, choir, and congregation begin with song. Our pastor has a special song or two, sometimes three.

Our church is not big and fancy, nor do we have the words to the songs we sing on the wall. We use a book on the back of the pews called the Church Hymnal. Some of the songs we sing are songs I remember from long ago, and they bring tears to my eyes more today than they did then.

Now it's time for the pastor to preach the sermon. As we are listening, I sit and look at the open doors, then down the aisle and at our pastor behind the pulpit. I look at the people on both sides of the church and watch them make their way to the altar, where they find help, love, and salvation. I find myself in the altar as well, in the need of help and understanding.

There are times when Jesus comes in and loves on his people while we worship him. Some of us weep, some pray, others testify of who he is and what he has done for us while we are living in this troubled world.

Every visitor is made welcome, and we are so happy to see them there. So, come on down for a visit and find help and love from the one who really cares, in our fair haven.

This little church is where I long to be, with my family and friends gathered closely beside me, while we live in this troubled world.

For I know who holds the future and I know who holds my hand

My Fair Haven

I feel so blessed to be able to get into my car
And drive to my fair haven just to be a part of this fair haven,
Where the people are beautiful and full of love
Each one is special in their own way I love each one
In this Haven there is charity, kindness and purity
There is instruction, warnings and protection
To protect us from a shipwreck in the stormy seas
It is a place of peace and holiness
Where Jesus visits with us.
Our haven of rest is in
Jesus

Spending time with Jesus makes a difference.

Jesus Saves

He left the splendor of Heaven
Where He was the Son of God
To come to a land and people
To be the Lamb that saves the lost

They hurt Him and they bruised Him
Then nailed him to a cross
They watched His blood flow down
As He was paying the cost

Jesus asked the Father to forgive them
For they know not what they do
And dropped His head and died
Paying the sin debt for me and you

They placed His body in a tomb
But it did not stay
He arose from the dead in three days
And the debt was fully paid

While He hung on the cross beside a thief
He forgave him of all his sins
Then took him to paradise
To spend eternity with him

While He was sitting at a well
He talked with a woman there
He knew everything about her
And forgave her sins as well

Once there was a teenager
Who had lost all her hope
She cried, dear Lord please forgive me
And keep me very close

Now He knows all about you
And all your inner most secrets
Just ask Him to forgive you and wash your sins away
He loves you very dearly and wants to hear you say
I believe

The time is drawing nigh
This thing is coming to an end
He will be returning
And our eternity will be with Him
"Come to Jesus today."

There's Evil in the Land

Christmas is over, decorations are put away, and we have a new year. It is time for ice, snow, and cold weather in the North Georgia Mountains. It is time for hurrying home, to stay warm, secure, and preparing for power outages. It is time for making plans for the New Year with our church, family, friends, and work. But all is not well, there is an evil in the land.

We have guns in our homes and in our possession. The news on the television and Internet show the bad things that are happening in the land.

This once was a land of the free, the home of the brave, and in God we trust. Nowadays, there is no trust. We lock our doors and look away, not making eye contact as we pass by. We sleep while bad things happen to children.

We have taken Bibles and God out of schools and keep them away from our children, not sharing our testimonies nor the love of God. Now, we wonder how this madness will end.

But there is a God in heaven who has the master plan. It is written in his word and on that you can depend.

Come to him genuinely and humbly to turn our nation around.

The Manual of Life

We hold it in our hands and press it to our heart. We kiss the pages with our love because we know the author is the one from above.

We read it from the front to back and pull words out from here and there. We study, meditate, and memorize, then hide them in our hearts.

We share them when we can to help save a lost soul or to mend a broken heart. These words are an anchor in mist of our storms. They are the lifeline that we hold to. While they tell us we will make it through.

The words are alive and speak to our hearts. They wash over our soul and give us a new start. They bring tears to our eyes and softens the hardest of hearts with a love that will never grow old. We find light for our path and order for our feet that's perfect in every detail.

The words in red are from our Savior—to teach us how to love one another and to never waver.

It has been handed down through the ages. The tears from the dear saints before have stained all the pages.

So, love it, cherish it, and pass the words on down, because there's a world full of people who need to hear words that are sound.

It holds our past, present, and future among its pages, while we wait and hide ourselves in the precious rock of ages.

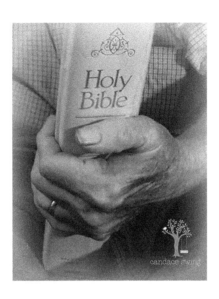

Our most valuable possession is the Word of God.

The picture above is titled "Daddy's Hands"

The grass withereth, the flower fadeth: but the
word of our God shall forever stand…

The Treasure Chest

Some days you open it
And the rubies, emeralds and jewels of all kind, pour out
Then there are days you have to pick and pick at it
Digging for the treasure
And you find a nugget, the nugget of wisdom.
This treasure chest is full
Of all the treasures you will ever need in life
This treasure chest is called, The Bible

"Keep the words before your eyes."

This poem came from my pastor's Wednesday night sermon.

Blessings

Through the years, we get caught up in working and providing for our families and loved ones. We take care of everyone and everything around us because that is what we do. Each one is truly precious blessings from God! But we become so devoted and caught up in them that we overlook the most precious blessings.

These most precious blessings are spiritual things. These spiritual things are experiencing the presence of God and the power of God. We can talk to the God who created the universe who has blessed us with all heavenly blessings in Christ. We can talk to his dear son, Jesus.

To become closer to God and to learn more about him, we can read his book. His book is exciting and thrilling. It tells us and shows us what he can do.

The language and knowledge that is found in this book is of God and not of man. This book is a spiritual blessing and has been overlooked as well.

So, pick it up, and get closer to God through his word, the Bible!

Photo By Candace Swing

The Shepherd and the Sheep

I have a friend whose name is Pam. She, her husband, Jack, and her parents went on vacation in the summer of two thousand nineteen.

While on their vacation and traveling through the state of Wyoming, they came upon a large heard of sheep, crossing the road in front of their van. She said there were sheep as far as she could see in the distance.

While waiting for the sheep to finish crossing, Pam decided to get out of the van and walk closer to the sheep to take a picture of them.

As she was walking toward them, she saw one dog watching over and protecting the whole heard of sheep. This dog let her know that she should get back into the van and she diligently complied.

As she showed me the pictures and told me about the sheep and the dog, my mind was remembering our Good Shepherd and how he takes care of all his sheep. The Good Shepherd gave his life for all the lost sheep in the world.

Jesus is the Good Shepherd
And you maybe a lost sheep wondering in the wilderness.
Come to the Good Shepherd,
He is waiting to care for you…

Jesus said, "My sheep hear my voice, and I know
them and they follow me and I give
unto them eternal life, and they shall never perish,
neither shall any man pluck them out of my hand."
Please come to Jesus today.

The Meeting

One Sunday morning, while sitting quietly in church and patiently waiting for the service to begin, someone sat down beside me and handed me several papers. I read the top page but was not understanding what it was saying. So, I continued to read it a couple more times before going on to the next page.

While reading the next page, the tears start to fill my eyes. I can feel the touch of Jesus now. This page contains the names and personal information of two people on it. They are a husband and a wife, serving as missionaries in a far country. They have been there for eighteen years.

I looked at their birthdays and anniversary. I know how old they are and how long they have been married. I try to picture what they look like. Jesus is still touching my heart but in a different way now. I can't move on to the next page. I'm getting to know these two people in my heart. These two very special people named Tommy and Lori.

The service begins, and I fold the papers and place them in my bag. It is a good service. Jesus is with us this morning. But, I feel like someone has given me a very special gift, and I have only read the first two pages.

Later in the day, I was able to finish reading the pages. The pages were prayer letters from the missionary. They told of what God is doing in this far country with these two people and other people. But the one that stood out the most to me was the one about the children.

Tommy and Lori have children church every Saturday. These services are held in a sixteen-foot shipping container with forty to fifty children each service. They are packed in it like sardines, says Tommy. The temperature gets very hot in the container.

However, week after week, the children continue to come. They learn to sing unto the Lord, hear Bible stories, and learn of Jesus the savior of the world! Many have been saved and some seem to be growing in the Lord.

But Tommy and Lori's hearts break for the children, and they pray they all will be saved. At that point, I'm crying. What a gift the Lord has given me. It is so special; I can hardly tell my husband about the children and these two people because the tears start to come.

The next day at work, I can't keep quiet. I want to tell everyone what someone has given me. But each time I talk about them, the tears fill my eyes again.

I have not met these to special people in person, but I love them and love what they are doing. If only I could tell them and let them know.

For the Children

Broken and weeping, in a dark place
They don't know who to trust, don't know their way
Your heart is breaking because you can't go to them
Jesus knows what to do and how to reach them
He has special people, who goes where he sends
He knows every child and knows how to mend.
So please remember Tommy and Lori, please remember these children
For they need you to help and to pray for them
Cry for the children…

All honor, glory and praise to the Lamb that
was slain for the sins of the world.

"The Rescue"

Lost, broken and stranded, they don't know the way. Just one wrong move and they will forever drift away. They are hanging on the best way they can, without any hope nor eternal plans.

There has to be someone to rescue them and bring them to the shore. Then tell them about Jesus and His grace galore.

But, the sea is raging and it seems no one wants to go. Still, there are a few whom Jesus well knows. Who will pursue the course no matter what comes their way, through the darkest of night with no light of day.

Though the sea winds are blowing and the waves are so strong. These rescuers are of a good courage and God helps them along.

They reach out to the lost and hurting and pull them on board. Without any care for themselves nor how far it is to shore.

Now everyone is exhausted and barely hanging on. As the sea captain continues steering with all of his might. Then there in the distance in the darkest of night. They see the light of Jesus glowing and He is waiting to hold them tight.

"Rescue the perishing, care for the dying, Jesus is merciful, Jesus will save"

Jesus Still Speaks

Once upon a time, in the year of 1977, my family went through a very difficult loss. My little sister, whose name was Penny, and at the age of eleven, went to be with Jesus.

At that time, I didn't know a lot about Jesus but believed in him with my whole heart.

The day before she went to heaven, Jesus spoke to me in an audible voice. I heard him loud and clear. There was no mistaking it. I understand that some people will not believe this, but it's true, and it happened. Like I said earlier, it was a very difficult time.

A few years later, the time came for me to share this experience with a pastor friend who was having a difficult time. I didn't tell him about hearing Jesus's voice, only what happened to my family and the things Jesus did.

When the conversation was over, and I was leaving, I asked the Lord if I had done the right thing sharing with him about what had happened. The Lord answered in an audible voice, "I gave it to you, use it."

Now, in the year of 2019, the Lord has answered another question.

The people, who really know me, know that I like to write. About a month ago, I asked the Lord to give me a new story. The next day, someone very special, being my mother, told me a story that happened to her many years ago and wanted it to be written for others to know, which I did just for her. But shortly after finishing the story. I became hesitant about sharing it with anyone.

Finally, asking the Lord if it was the right thing to do with this story, he answered a second time with the same exact words, in an audible voice, "I gave it to you, use it."

Just those few words mean everything to me. No more questioning, nor worrying, if I had said the right words or done the right thing. It was settled within my heart. The voice of Jesus takes care of it all.

Jesus is still loving and intimate with his children today. For those of you who don't believe, just know that Jesus and His word is the same today as it was years ago. He never changes. He is still real today. He wants a genuine relationship with you too.

Please come to Jesus today.

The One who spoke the stars into place and
the moon that shines at night.
The One who spoke and the land and waters were formed,
Then made man with pure delight,
The One who came to earth in the flesh,
Whose words are of power and life
I wonder how He could speak His words
To someone as lowly as I...

Ripples of Love

When Jesus dips his finger into your heart, the moment he touches it, oh the joy that fills your heart. He makes his presence known and is face to face with you as he dips his finger into your heart.

You're in his presence now. The joy that fills your heart is beyond compare. Oh, the love, strength, and power that's all around, when Jesus reaches in and touches your heart.

When Jesus dips his finger into your heart, it is like a pebble dropped into a pool of water and the ripples flow outwardly.

As he touches the center of your heart, the joy and love ripples outward until your heart is completely filled. Then it ripples to your face, bringing the best smile you have ever smiled in your whole life. The love continues rippling outwards, touching other people, souls, and hearts. Who knows how far a ripple of Jesus's love will travel?

If I could paint you a picture to show you this touch, it would not show the depth of joy that actually touches your heart.

If I searched the whole world over to find something or some-one to show you this touch, still it would not show the depth of joy and love that his touch brings into your heart.

Only Jesus can touch your heart like this.

Ask Jesus to come into your heart.

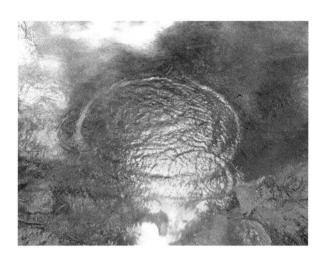

The picture was taken at Anna Ruby Falls in Helen, Georgia, while we were visiting the falls our granddaughter, tossed a pebble into the water. While we watched the ripples flowing outward, I was able to take a picture.

He touched me oh the joy that floods my soul
Something happened and now I know
He touched me and made me whole…

Dancing with Jesus

One Sunday morning in February 2020, while getting ready for church, my mind was thinking only of Jesus. I began praying and asking him to please allow me to experience his presence in a big way during the morning service.

While driving to church, the thoughts of Jesus lingered in my heart and mind until I noticed the church's parking lot was overflowing with vehicles, and most of them were trucks. However, I found a place to park on the grassy area and made my way to the sanctuary, where I said hello to several people, and had a seat on the back row.

Shortly, the choir and congregation began to sing. Just a few moments after the music started, the Lord touched me in a big way. He is so awesome!

While sensing His Holy Spirit behind me, he touched both my arms, while drawing me behind the pew. His spirit seemed to be happy and dancing. He really liked our church music and was happy being there.

I sat there silently, not knowing whether to move or be still. Then it felt as though I could leap over the back of the pew. It was amazing! At that moment and weeks after, there didn't seem to be any words to use to help share this experience with anyone.

Jesus' touch is so beautiful and beyond anything that anyone could imagine. It will be treasured in my heart forever and some-day—whether here in this life or in Heaven, I do not know—I will "dance with Jesus," and not sit silently in my seat any longer.

Do You Know this Man?

It was the Friday before Easter in a busy little town when an unexpected scene got our attention. It was a man, carrying a large wooden cross upon his shoulder, down his back, and on to the ground as he walked along the side of the road. While watching him pass by, I questioned, who is that man?

The man, carrying the cross was signifying Jesus, our Savior, being tortured and carrying the cross that he was to be nailed upon and his blood that flowed down. This should have been enough to humble a Christian to the point of falling to their knees in prayer.

Then remembering his resurrection and ascension into heaven where he sits at the right hand of the Father. Should have been enough to raise a Christian up with his hands lifted high, in honor and worship and praise unto Christ Jesus the King while the Holy Spirit revived us again.

And it should have been enough for the lost, who were watching with the Christians, to come to the saving knowledge of Jesus Christ as the Holy Spirit touched their heart and drew them to Christ.

The man continued to drag the cross as he walked down the side of the road until he was out of sight. Now, my question is, do you know Jesus?

He is so much more than just a man.
Our greatest need is to be born again.

Come and Dine

Everyone wants to hear someone say
I love you
I love you with all my heart
Then we mess up badly and so sorry we did
All we want to hear is someone to say
I forgive you
Do you remember when you were a child
and playing outside all afternoon?
Then evening would begin to draw nigh
You would listen for your mother's cry
Come and get it
It's supper time
We all want to hear these words throughout our lives
There is one who has said them all
I love you
I forgive you
Come and dine with me
Jesus

If you want real joy
Love Jesus first
Love others second
And love you third
Jesus, Others, You
That spells
Joy.

Hearts of Every Kind

Hearts, flowers, cards, and balloons
Valentine candies, dinner, and looking at the moon
Hearts full of love and broken ones too
This is what we see on Valentine's Day;
There is one whose love ran red
For hearts of every kind
With heights of love beyond compare
Want you set your mind;
You can be His and He can be yours
And forever you shall be
Bought with a price, not of silver nor gold
But with the precious blood of Thee
Jesus Christ

Want you be Mine

For God so loved the world, that He gave his only begotten Son, that whosoever believeth in him should not perish, but have ever lasting life. (John 3:16)

Salvation is a heart thing, not a mind thing.

Belonging

In the world today, it is hard to completely belong
to or to be intimate with someone.
Someone that you can completely trust with your whole
heart and be not afraid of them harming you in some way.
Or someone who only wants the best for you.
But there is one who hears your heart when
you don't say anything at all.
Whether it is broken or full of love. He hears
every sigh, He hears every word.
Then He speaks to your heart and says,
I am yours, you are mine Forever we shall be
Sealed with a seal that cannot be broken
Throughout eternity
Jesus
"If you will only believe."

Trusting

Have you ever been in God's presence or stood still while His spirit was all around you and over you?

Did the thought ever come to your mind, there has to be a God? Because man does not have the knowledge to do nor the ability to create this thing.

Have you ever been protected when something was about to harm you and later realized it was God?

Have you ever wondered, how did I make it through that and still be here, then think it's got to be God?

Have you ever thought about Heaven and eternal life with Jesus? This is real.

Has there been one time in your whole life when you bowed on your knees and asked Jesus to forgive you of your sins and to come into your heart?

It only takes one time, you will always be His…

Heaven and eternal life is as close as the words
I believe.

Once you are Mine, you're always Mine.

The Uniform

'Twas the middle of winter, early one Saturday morning, before the light of day, when a firm knock echoed from the front door. Our little granddaughter and I were in the bedroom. Jim and our four-month-old grandson were in the living room.

The sound of adult male voices came from the living room. My heart knew who it was. So, I entered the room to say hello.

In the middle of the room, in the dim lights, stood a tall, large, stern looking man in a dark uniform. You could not tell who he was, only that he was a police officer in full uniform.

I looked at him and said hello, then turned and left the room, to continue preparing for my day. Shortly returning one more time to see the person in our living room even though my heart still knew who he was.

The police officer had been on patrol all night, watching over the citizens of the county. He never speaks of what he does, what he sees, or what he goes through while on his job. He looks so big and strong. The thickness of the protective wear makes him appear much larger than he really is. But I know underneath all the layers of the uniform there is a caring and sensitive and loving man.

I looked into the dimly lit room. There sitting in the recliner was this large police officer, holding his four-month-old little boy and feeding him his baby bottle. My heart melted as I looked at him because this police officer, holding his little baby so lovingly and tenderly, is my son.

Pray for our police officers.

If That Isn't Love
(Excerpt)

Jesus left the splendor of heaven, knowing His destiny;
Was the lonely hill of Golgotha; there to lay down His life for me…
Even in death He remembered, the thief hanging by His side;
Then he spoke of love and compassion and He took him to paradise
And if that isn't love; then the ocean is dry;
There's no stars in the sky and the little sparrows can't fly;
If that isn't love; then heaven's a myth;
There's no feeling like this;
If that isn't love

There were three crosses on the hill that day.

Share a Little Kindness

Wherever you go, from day to day
Be kind to someone along the way
Treat every day as if it were a gift
To cherish and love someone
That will certainly give you both a lift;
However and wherever your life may lead
Take a little time to give a gentle smile
Or touch someone's hand,
Just one kind gesture can help someone
More than you may understand;
Then reach out and find the way
To tell them about Jesus
His amazing love and saving grace
For this is the day
For someone to be saved
Share the love of Jesus today

In Memory of Ernie
July 26, 2018

Words, Words, Everywhere Words

Some make our hearts smile
And some make us cry
Some are full of compassion and love
And some are full of pride

Some are caring, gentle and kind
And some are made in haste
Some we are required to say
While others we wish we had never said

There are words that are taken the wrong way
And we may never know
What they really wanted to say

Whatever the word maybe, from out of the heart they come
So be careful what you say
For we shall give account for them some day.

God's People

There was a time when I passed through a small country town in North Georgia. To look at it, you would think it was just a regular small town with not much happening.

In spite of that, I decided to stop and spend some time there. What I found was, this little town had many of God's people living and working there.

Families and friends, churches and homes, businesses and establishments, everyone living and loving, and some struggling and needing just a kind word to help them along.

While I was there, people took me in. They showed kindness, friendship, and love. When I was wrong, they corrected me. When I was right, they were happy. When I was sick, they prayed. They gave me more than I could ever give them in return. Each one was special in their own way.

When it was time to leave, I realized how precious and amazing these people have been. Not only to me, but to all the other people who come through their door.

Thank you, my friends! What a true blessing you are!

> *For I am with thee, and no man shall set on thee to*
> *hurt thee: for I have much people in this city.*
> —Acts 18:10

Chapter 3

Ask, Seek, and Knock

The Voice of Love

Behold, I stand at the door, and knock: **if any man hear my voice**, and open the door, I will come in to him, and will sup with him, and he with me. (Rev.3:20)

Just open your heart's door, I will come in and dine with you. I will fellowship with you. I will come into your life and transform it. I will love you in a way that you have never been loved before. What I begin with you will never end. Our relationship will be eternal.

Hear my voice,
My voice of love.
Jesus

Knocking on Heaven's Door

Around six o'clock one Sunday morning, the phone rings. We check the caller ID to see who is calling so early. But it isn't a number Jim and I recognize, cautiously, I say hello.

The caller replied with a very weak and low voice. It said, "Mom I'm in the hospital." I have heart failure and kidney failure. Then the same weak voice gives me the name of the hospital. My reply was, "We will be there shortly."

It is an hour and a half drive to the hospital. As Jim drove, I sat there in silence with my heart, breaking inside of me and not knowing what to expect when we arrive.

As we entered his room, the only person or thing my eyes could focus on was my child, now a grown man and sicker than he has ever been before.

We watched him struggling to live and the doctors working so hard on him. I felt as though I was going to fall completely apart, while thinking this can't be happening.

I stood closely by his side, caressing his head and hands, not being able to move away from him. Every minute, every hour, by his side is where I had to be.

While rubbing his head and looking into his face, I was taken back about thirty-seven years—to a time when I stood closely by my little boy's bedside in the hospital and rubbing his little head then. A tiny little boy that had surgery and my heart was hurting so badly for him then.

Now a grown man and my heart hurting so badly that I can't explain it to you. I think I may scream. Scared I can't control the crying and afraid of losing control of myself, I remain quite while rubbing his head and whispering, "Jesus, Jesus, Jesus."

I am here, talking and listening to doctors and nurses. I'm standing and looking at them while touching and caressing my child's head and hands.

We got through Sunday. Sunday night, we didn't sleep. I watched as he struggled to live. Oh, God, please help my son.

Monday, doctors and nurses still trying to figure out what happened. They start dialysis. The nurse whispers, I don't think he will make it through if you're not with him. They slip me in the dialysis room. I stay closely by his side and watch as his blood comes out of his body. Then it's over, and we go back to his room. Can't close my eyes, afraid he may stop breathing. Must watch for next breath to come. Family come in and out, talking and watching. I cry…

Tuesday, doctors and nurses working. Blood pressure, heart, breathing, kidneys not working. He is so sick. More dialysis. He cries, I continue to watch for next breath and cry.

Wednesday, doctors and nurses are so awesome. I go to cafeteria for breakfast alone. Get my food, pay for it, and sit down. I look at the food and start crying.

Our pastor comes today. He steps out of the elevator, and I look at him and cry. He visits for a while and talks with my son. He prays, and I pray too.

Thursday, doctors say he didn't have a heart attack. I can see a change in his breathing, a change in his face and a change in his voice. I stand in the elevator with the door closed and cry.

Friday, they are going to move him from ICU to a regular room today. I am so happy! An hour later, the results of the biopsy of his kidneys come back. They will never work again, and he will be on dialysis three days a week the rest of his life. He cries, I hold him tight. I cry.

Saturday, he is looking good, and he is becoming his self again. Thank you, Jesus, for holding us through this week. I cry.

Sunday morning, he didn't sleep well, but he is doing much better. I have to leave him now. I will return in four days. Family are going to take care of him now. I cry…

God holds our breath in His hands.
November 22, 2015

Hold On to Your Faith

When the storm is ragging, keep your eyes on Jesus. He will help you. Don't doubt Him.

There will be some tough times to come along, but don't take your eyes off Jesus and his word.

He knows your praying. He hears every word. Don't give up because he hasn't answered. Sometimes, we are not ready for his answer. Don't let the devil still your faith.

During the hard times when you are hurting, don't forget he loves you. He is right there with you.

Keep your eyes on Christ, even though you can barely see him through your tears. He will never leave you that is a promise he gave you when you accepted him and believed.

You are his child. He created you and loves you. He knows how your heart feels. He knows how your body feels. He knows every hair on your head. He knows what you are thinking right now.

Your life maybe filled with sickness and pain. But with
Jesus there is healing and hope. And every day will be
a little better because you have been with Him.
Be not afraid, only believe.

Ask Me About My Son

January 16, 2016

Donna, how's your son?
Ahh… The doctor gave him good news.
He said, something is working double.
They don't know if it is the medicine, the dialysis or his kidneys.
The doctor said, don't get your hopes up.
Then they cut his intake of medicine in half.
May take six months to figure out what is going on.
My son said, "I don't have to worry about dying every day now,
    Mom."
Lord, thank you with all my heart,
I love you!

> *Child of God, no matter what you are going*
> *through, Jesus is still in control.*

What Is Going On?

April 2017

The phone begins to ring again. I wonder who this could be calling and say hello. An excited voice says, "Hey Mom!" Doctors say they have never seen anything like it. One doctor said that it is a miracle. I am so happy!

They want to do another biopsy and run some more test to find out what is going on? Doctor said, "I don't need dialysis anymore." They said this just doesn't happen. "I'm so happy, Mom." "It's because of your prayers, Mom.:

> *But, this mom knows that it is you Jesus.*
> *Thank you again, Lord.*
>
> *So, let us give God the glory*
> *And give Him all of our praise!*

It has been almost three years since my son became sick. He does not need dialysis at this time. His kidneys are functioning on their own. His blood pressure is stable. Doctors can't explain this.

No matter what the problem, God is still right there with you. Sometimes, the road is hard and long. He never said it would be easy. But, he did say, he would never leave us. It may not be the answer we want, but he will love us with an everlasting love through it.

Praise Jesus

Christian no matter what the sickness or problem is
That you are going through, Jesus is with you.
No matter what is going on inside your body
Praise your way through
While loving Him and praising him,
He will be loving on you

Even though this sickness is the hardest thing you ever had to do
It breaks your heart completely
While you watch the ones you love hurting too
Continue to praise Jesus for He is holding you

When your body is filled with pain
And you can't raise your hands, nor call out His name
He hears your hearts cry and holds you in His hands.
Oh, praise His holy name
For He understands

He will never ever leave you
He will stay until the end
Then take you to glory to spend eternity with Him
Where you can praise Him forever and never hurt again

You'll be worshiping and singing, walking on streets of gold
Shouting and praising, and never growing old
And doing it all in the presence of our Lord and Saviour
Oh praise Jesus any way you can…

In memory of a friend.
2019

The Bouquet

As the rose in the rose of Sharon and the lily in the Lily of the Valley, represents our Lord Jesus Christ, the flowers in the bouquet of life represents the family and friends the Lord has picked from around the world and given to each of us.

Each one is a rare and delicate flower grown with the master gardener's hands. First, we find the flower of a faithful spouse, next are the flowers of a loving family, then the flowers of true friends. All tied together in one arrangement.

They have the sweet aroma of loyalty and faithfulness. They are arrayed in beautiful colors, shapes, and sizes. Some may have a broken petal or two, or a withered leaf, still they bloom within our hearts and lives all through the years.

Each one holds a special place in this bouquet. When one flower fades and is pulled from the bouquet, its aroma and beauty remains in our heart and mind until we meet again in the Master's home.

He Knows

When you're far away and I can't be there
I will be on my knees praying a prayer;
When you're sick and hurting and the doctors can't help
I will be on my knees pleading for God to help;
When you're all alone and lost all hope
I will fall on my knees weeping for Jesus to be close;
Then He reaches into my heart and takes you and all these things
        out of me
And holds them his hands;
If you should grow weak and can no longer stand;
You will be cradled in His arms and held tight in His hands;
For He knows all your tears and knows all your fears
He has known you right from the start
But most of all my dear, He knows you by your heart.

It's in the Savior's Hands
(Excerpt)

Oh, it's in the Savior's hands, those precious nail-scarred hands.
I may not understand, I'm trusting in the Great I Am.
It's good to know it's in the Savior's hands.
Though driven through with nails, those
precious hands, they'll never fail.
I may not understand, I'm trusting in the Great I am.
It's good to know it's in the Savior's hands.

*And ye shall seek me, and find me, when ye
shall search for me with all your heart.*
—Jeremiah 29:13

Prayer Changes Things

Once a month, on a Friday morning. everyone arrives early for our meeting. As we gather together in the lobby, there is a sense of genuine care and faithfulness among the people.

I usually sit on the fireplace hearth with two or three ladies. The rest of the team sit on chairs or on the sofa in a semicircle around the room. Our leader stands in front of us, and the meeting begins. We never know what he is going to say or do.

In this particular meeting, the special things come first. Breakfast is served!

Next, our leader speaks about what the Lord has done and is doing in our lives and for others. We follow him with prayer requests for the ones who need help or healing. Whether it is a customer, family, friends or ourselves, we share with the group.

We stand and huddle into a circle. While holding hands, we begin to pray. This is where our strength, help, and unity come from. God has put these special people together for this place and time.

When the prayer time is over, while wiping the tears from our eyes, we return to our seat and our leader begins the next part of our meeting.

He shares all the business matters with us, employees are recognized for their accomplishments, and anniversaries and birthdays are acknowledged as well. We all listen and watch each one as they smile and enjoy themselves. Occasionally, we just do something fun and everyone joins in the activity.

Now, our time is up, and we are ready to start the day with joy and love in our hearts, to share with our customers and each other. It is awesome just being a part of this meeting!

Jesus said, Again I say unto you, That if two of you shall agree on earth as touching anything that they shall ask, it shall be done for them of my Father which is in heaven.

For where two or three are gathered together in my name, there am I in the midst of them. (Matt. 18:19–20).

If you don't quit, he won't quit.

Pray about Everything

Once, there was a man. He suffered greatly from a certain disability. When he spoke, his words were loud and of great need. He would look at me and loudly say, "Pray for me! Pray about everything!"

This man came by once or twice every month. Each time was the same as the time before. While looking at me, he would say in a loud, desperate tone of voice, "Pray for me! Pray for my family, pray about everything!"

Each time, I looked back at him and replied, "I will."

It has been over three years sense I have seen this man. But the memory of his face and his words remain with me still. *Pray for me! Pray about everything!* Now I find I'm praying about everything.

Thank you, Lord, for everything

In the Throne Room

If your life is a total wreck
You don't know what to do
Run to the Savior
He is waiting just for you
There is a place we can run
Where there is never a crowd
And the cares of your heart will be heard
Run to the Savior
As fast as you can
It does not matter how many of His children are calling Him
He knows your voice as if you were His only child
Run to Jesus
In His throne room of grace
He is waiting to hear from you…

Go With God

Our God is a big God. If you follow his lead, he will bless you—even though to everyone's eyes, you're making a mistake and they shake their head at your decision.

If you continue to follow him, he will bless you in ways you would have never known if you had stood still. It may not be with prestige and wealth of the world—instead it will be with a far greater kind.

When it is over, you will look back on where you have been, what you have seen, and experienced. All you will be able to say is that was God. Then look at where he has led you now, and you will say, "This is still God!"

He is a good God. He will never lead you down the wrong road. He knows your beginning and your end. Follow God…

I believe I will go with God.

The Broken Servant

Only you Lord know what a servant's heart is feeling without them saying a word.

When down on their knees and the tears start to flow, not a word comes from their mouth—still you hear every word, you know every hurt.

When a servant's heart is fainting and whispers your name, you hear every whisper, and you hear every sigh.

When their heart has grown feeble and their mouth cannot speak, you know when it happens and give them your strength.

It's in times like these when others don't know that brings us closer to you.

When we are alone with you, you hold our heart in your hands and help us loose our self in you.

While we commune with you without saying a word.

He must increase and I must decrease.

Chapter 3

Gifts from God

The Gender

My husband and I have been married forty years. Throughout the years, we have had children, grandchildren, and great grandchildren.

Actually, I've had the privilege of witnessing the birth of a grandson. During his birth, the doctor asked if I wanted to cut the cord? Naturally, I said no and told him he could do it.

Sad to say, we had one grand baby to go to heaven way too early. But we know he is cradled in the arms of Jesus as we speak.

There were two specific times when the Lord allowed me to know what gender the baby was before anyone else could know. Both times, it was too early for the doctors to see if they were male or female.

The first time was in the year of 2000—we received word that we were going to have a new grandbaby. It was not our first grandchild. Still, I was excited, as if it was the first.

I wanted to do something extra special for this baby. So, I decided to start a baby quilt and hoped to have it ready when the baby arrived, but there was one small problem. I didn't know whether to make it for a boy or girl?

The morning after the announcement, I woke to a beautiful spring morning with the sun shining through the bedroom window. While making my bed, I began to pray about the new baby and the quilt. By the time I had finished making the bed, I knew to make it for a girl.

When the baby arrived, she was named "Samantha," and she had a brand-new quilt.

Sixteen years later, our youngest son and his wife came over and told us they were going to have a baby. We were so excited. But again, it was too early for the doctors to see if it was a boy or girl.

We talked awhile, and they left to go to their home. The moment the door closed behind them, the Lord showed me a tiny baby boy. Immediately, I told my husband it's a boy! It seemed to be a long seven or eight months because not everyone believed me when I told them the baby was a boy. Some people just looked at me, not knowing what to say.

When the baby arrived, he was named "Wyatt."

The purpose of this story is to let you know, Jesus loves and knows each tiny baby personally. They are alive at conception. He then forms them together in their mother's womb, making them male and female.

You can rest assured when God makes a baby a boy, he will always be a male. When he makes a baby a girl, she will always be a female. God makes no mistakes. He is God.

So, take care of the babies, Moms and Dads, from conception and beyond because God has entrusted you with them. He knows everything that happens to them.

Who Is the Greatest?

Who could be the greatest among us? Could it be our neighbor or a loved one? Could it be the president of the United States? Who could it be? Maybe an actor or singer? Who do you think the greatest person is?

In essence, the person that is the greatest is the least of us all—being the most humble and the least educated than anyone. This person is completely dependent on someone else to survive.

Maybe you question how could this be? The one that is the greatest among us is the least of all. This person has a tender and forgiving heart. This person is trusting and full of love, joy, and faith. You can see the love in their face and eyes when they look to you. They love you no matter what you do.

The greatest among us is the weakest and most innocent. This loving and trusting person thinks you're the greatest in the whole world and looks up to you.

This person doesn't know they are the greatest in Jesus's eyes. Most of the world doesn't know it either.

The greatest among us is a little child—a miracle from God. A child's faith and love alone is an open road straight to the heart of God.

Take care of our children, America.

At the same time came the disciples unto Jesus, saying, Who is the greatest in the kingdom of heaven?

And Jesus called a little child unto him, and set him in the midst of them,

And said, Verily I say unto you, Except ye be converted, and become as little children, ye shall not enter into the kingdom of heaven.

Whosoever therefore shall humble himself as this little child, the same is greatest in the kingdom of heaven.

And whoso shall receive one such little child in my name receiveth me.

But whoso shall offend one of these little ones which believe in me, it were better for him that a millstone were hanged about his neck, and that he were drowned in the depth of the sea. (Matt. 18:1–6)

Have you ever looked into a three-year-old's face when they closed their eyes and bowed their head in prayer? Have you ever listened closely to the words they were praying? Jesus has.
Red, yellow, black, or white
They are precious in His sight
Jesus loves the little children of the world

No one has yet realized the wealth of sympathy, kindness, generosity and tenderheartedness hidden in the soul and heart of a child.

God Creates Them Male and Female

There's a special place in heaven where all babies play—until it's time for them to come to Earth someday. God takes special care and knows each one then breathes the breath of life into each tiny one.

At conception, the babies are breathing and are being knitted together in their mother's womb. God makes no mistakes. He does this when no one else knows there is a new life on that day.

Oh, the love and care the Lord has with each tiny one. They are such precious little lives and very important to him. He knows everything about them. Sometimes, he will share the gender of a baby before anyone else can tell.

So, take care, Moms and Dads. Take care, America, of these tiny little babies because God knows what is happening to them.

> Thou didst knit me together in my mother's womb.
> —Psalm 139:13

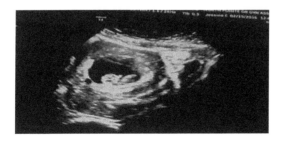

*Human life comes from God, in him we live,
move, and have our very being.*

The Father's Love

Can you think of a more wonderful place to be
Than cradled in your Father's hand?

No worrying about anyone or anything,
Nor anxiety, strife, or fear,
Because you know,
Your Father is holding you near

Oh, the peace and purity that will abound,
What comfort and love you have found
While you are held in your Father's hand

You will close your eyes and rest
Without any tears or stress
While you are laying in your Fathers hand

His hand is big and strong
And can hold you all night long;
So, close your eyes my child and rest
In your Father's hand

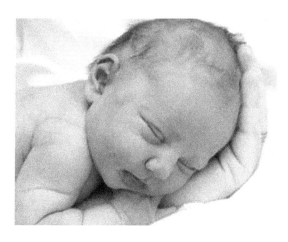

My sheep hear my voice, and I know them, and they follow me;
And I give unto them eternal life; and they shall never perish,
neither shall any man pluck them out of my hand.
My Father, which gave them me, is greater than all; and
no man is able to pluck them out of my Father's hand.
I and my Father are one.

—John 10:27–29

The Gift

Two little hands and two little feet
Ten little fingers and ten little toes

Two blue eyes
That are bright as the moon
With a smile on her face
That lights up a room

She's the happiest little girl
That is filled with
Trust and love…

A peaceful little angel
With a spirit
Gentle as a dove

Such a priceless little gift
From the Father above
Given to us
To cherish and love

This little granddaughter of ours
Pennie

Cry For the Children

Broken and weeping, in a dark place
They don't know who to trust, don't know their way
Your heart is breaking because you can't get to them
Cry out to Jesus today
Jesus can get to them when no one else can
Faith is strong, stronger than man
Your faith is going to help them when all else fails
Cry out to Jesus today
Your family is your priority
The world wants to steal them and take them away
You must point them to Jesus, get them to Him to stay
Cry out to Jesus today
So, keep your faith strong, as strong as you can
Your faith cometh by hearing, and hearing by the word of God
While you keep on believing and holding to His hand
Cry for the children today…

Chapter 4

Always Faithful

Time

When she was young, she had black hair. She stood with her back straight and a smile on her face.

She loved her husband, son, and daughter. She loved her mom and dad, sisters and brother. She loved going back home for a visit with them and all the others.

I watched her get ready for work, make her clothes, and do her nails. She taught me how to make teacakes even though I still can't do it very well.

Now, her hair is gray, and she falls along the way. She seems to forget more and more with each passing day.

But in the heart of her two grandsons, she is loved now more than ever.

♥

Jesus Christ knew you when your heart was young
And he knows you now
He loved you then, and he loves you now

Mamma's Faith

Mamma has exemplified faith in the presence of her children all their lives. She knew the Word of God and He helped her many times. One of the times he helped her was with the birth of my little sister, Pamela.

Pam was born in the year of 1970. She was the most beautiful, red haired little girl anyone had ever seen. There was one little problem. She was born with a disability. This disability was a club foot, meaning the bottom of her foot was turned completely upside down.

Mom started as early as possible to correct this for her baby girl. So when she grew she would be able to walk normally. But, this would be a hard and long process for both of them.

It started with multiple surgeries, wearing casts, special shoes with braces and a brace on her leg. Pam grew and started to walk. I remember her walking with her cast on. I also remember her walking with the special shoes on. This pair of shoes had a metal bar that ran from one shoe to the other to connect them. She was determined to walk and Mom was making sure she did.

I remember riding Gray Hound buses to doctor appointments with them at Scottish Rite Hospital in Atlanta, Ga. I also remember the Shriners picking us up and taking us to the hospital to help her be able to walk.

Then it finally happened, the little girl was walking and going to school. One foot was a size smaller than the other one. But, that was ok. Because she was walking.

Pam grew and was very talented. She played the piano and sang so beautifully. When she was 13 she was playing and singing in church with mom in the congregation. This particular time she got up from the piano and started down the aisle. Then without any warning, she fell flat on the floor.

The women in the congregation all ran to her. They shouted, someone call an ambulance. But, mom was trying to get to her daughter. She said, "Let me through, I need to get to her" She knelt down beside her and asked, what's wrong? Pam said, "It's my foot. It quit working."

Mom said, at that moment everything that she had done for Pam passed before her eyes. Then she said, "No, this isn't happening!" She then laid her hand on Pam and said, "In the name of Jesus Christ of Nazareth, The Son of The Living God, you will walk." Pam got up and finished walking down the aisle by herself. Now being a grown woman with children of her own, she hasn't had any more problems walking with her foot.

God is so good!

Momma's Heart

Mom spoke of a time when she was a single mother and her children were young. A time when I did not realize what she was going through all alone.

She said it had been difficult raising her children without enough money to care and provide for them.

Then the time came when she realized she couldn't care for them any longer. Being desperate, she came to the conclusion, that she had to make a decision.

The next morning, she awoke as normal and got her children ready for school. To be alone just for a moment, she went to the back porch and sat down on the doorsteps. She began to pray, "Lord, I can't take care them. I'm going to town, and I'm not coming back until I find a job".

When she finished praying, she got up and returned to her children. By then, it was time for the school bus to arrive. She kissed them goodbye, and they got on the bus.

As the bus pulled away, Mom turned and went back inside to begin getting ready for her plan when a knock on the front door echoed through the silent house.

She opened the door, and there stood a young man with his little boy. He knew Mom from watching her with her children in the neighborhood.

The young man asked, "Will you take care of my son while I work? I will pay you."

Mom looked at the young man and said, "Yes."

Then shortly, a knock came from the back door. Mom went to the door. It was a lady Mom knew. The lady asked, "Would you be interested in taking care of my little boy while I work? I will pay you."

Again, Mom said, "Yes."

And this was the beginning of Mom's Child Caring Business, which she did for many years to come. God is an awesome God and a right-on-time God!

Momma's Laughter

I love to see Momma smile and hear her laugh. Yesterday, she told me a story of something that happened years ago.

It was about a few ladies in a church where she was attending. These ladies were her friends, and they would call her quite frequently just to talk.

Every day, they would call one after the other. This went on for quite a while. But this one day, the phone rang, and she answered it. The lady began talking. While Momma was listening, the receiver that she held to her ear began to shock her ear. Tiny little shocks came from the phone. She told the lady she had to go because something was wrong with her telephone. She said goodbye and hung up the phone. Then Momma forgot all about the phone problem.

When the next lady called and started talking, the phone started the tiny shocks to her ear again. So, she told that lady the same and hung up the phone. Again, she forgot the problem with the phone and went about her daily routine.

Then the third lady called. Her name was Gladys. When she began talking, the phone started the tiny shocks. Mama told her she had to go. But Gladys said, "You need to get you a new phone." But Momma said goodbye and hung the phone up again.

This went on five or six times. Then one day, no one called. The phone did not ring. The ladies stopped calling. Momma didn't experience any more problems with her phone.

Then she started laughing as she finished telling the story.

She had realized that all the talking that was going on was only "gossip," and it had come to a complete stop. Mom continued to laugh.

We who would obey the Lord
And love our neighbor as He taught
Know well that it is deeply wrong
To pass a hurtful tale along,
When a single whisper's done
The tale is heard by everyone
Like a poison spreading through a ward
It sickens all
O GOSSIP NOT! (Author unknown)

Gossip is a person who habitually reveals personal or sensational facts about others.

Also known as one who reveals secrets, one who goes about as a talebearer. A gossiper is a person who has privileged information about someone and proceeds to reveal that information to those who have no business knowing it.

The Journey

Momma told me of a time many years ago when she encountered two bulldogs. One was a black male, and the other one was a white female. She said both were muscular and large dogs.

Every day, after Mom and her family finished their evening meal, she would take the leftover scraps from the table out to the fence in the back yard and left them there.

Down the road lived a family who owned the two bulldogs. The dogs would come to the fence and eat the scraps Mom had left there.

Time passed, and now Mom lives alone and no longer has the amount of scraps to take to the fence for the dogs. So, she didn't bother to do so any longer.

One evening, she went to the back door, and there stood the two dogs looking up at her. She returned to the kitchen, got the few scraps that she had left over, and gave it to the dogs.

The male dog would not eat. He stepped back and watched while the female ate. When she finished, he ate what was left.

The dogs kept coming every evening to the back door. After a while, they stopped coming. Mom found out the family had moved away and taken the dogs with them.

Approximately two months passed, one day, Mom's youngest son, Tim, was out back doing some yard work. She heard him call to her, "You have a visitor." She went to the back door, and there stood the black bulldog, all alone, looking up at her. All she had to feed him this time was half a pawn of corn bread. She broke it up for him, he ate every bite and stood there looking at her again.

Then Mom began to cry while she told me the rest of the story. She said he had large eyes, and they were blood shot, his body was thin, and he was worn down. She said there's no telling how far he had come just to get something to eat. She continued to cry.

At this point, Mom said she didn't know what this story would mean to anyone, and I didn't know what to say to her.

But I can tell you it doesn't matter if you're red, yellow, black or white, rich or poor, male or female, if you have been on a hard journey in this life and you need to find a place of solace and to be feed, come to Jesus.

For he is the Bread of Life. and you will never hunger again. He will give you living water, and you will never thirst again. He will give rest to your weary soul and will never leave you.

Come to Jesus.

Just One Touch

Momma told me of a trip she made long ago. A trip with her closest friend who she called Sister Ethel. Sister Ethel was in a wheelchair. Mom didn't say what was wrong with her. Only that Sister Ethel desired a touch from Jesus.

Sister Ethel had heard a certain preacher was going to be having meetings in South Georgia, and she wanted to attend one. She asked Mom to go with her. Mom agreed to go even though she had doubts about this preacher. When they arrived at the meeting, the place was packed with people. Mom and Sister Ethel had to sit in the back of the auditorium.

It was a very good service, and the Holy Spirit was moving. Sister Ethel wanted to go to the altar to be prayed for. So, Mom tried to get Sister Ethel there, but there were so many people she couldn't get her to the altar in the wheelchair. Finally, she was almost there, when she saw the Man of God starting to leave. Momma pushed Sister Ethel as hard as she good to get her there before he left. Fortunately, they were able to catch him before he got to the door.

The Man of God looked at the two women, and instead of praying for Sister Ethel, he reached out and prayed for Mom. The Holy Spirit touched Mom, and she hit the floor out cold. She didn't know how long she was out.

Then she began to tell me what she had seen while she was out.

She was in a dark tunnel. At the other end of the tunnel was a light. Then she heard someone speak to her. He said, "You have to go back."

Mom said, "I don't want to go back."

Again, he said, "You have to go back."

Again, Mom said, "I don't want to go back."

A third time, he said, "You have to go back."

Instantly, Mom was back and awake. Momma said she has never understood why God touched her and not Sister Ethel. Because she was the godliest person Mom had ever known.

But to me, my mom is the godliest person I have ever known.

Momma's Song

I used to go to church on Sunday Mornings
I would try to sing, pray and shout
To tell the truth about the Holy Spirit
I didn't know what it was all about
As I went to church on Sunday Morning
And the preacher made the alter call
I was guided by the Holy Spirit
And down on the altar I did fall
Now as I go to church on Sunday Morning
Jesus has a good plan all worked out
To tell the truth about the Holy Spirit
I know just what it's all about

The Holy Ghost will set your feet a dancing
The Holy Ghost will thrill you thru and thru
The Holy Ghost will set your feet a dancing
And your heart will be dancing too…

Forever

There are times I just need to praise you
And there are times I only cry
There are times I call your name out
And say thank you, while the people wonder why;
Sometimes I raise my hands in worship
Or bow my head and cry
Because your love surrounds me
And makes the world subside;
At times I whisper hallelujah and then shout amen
When you give me a glimpse of your glory
And of a city with no end;
There are times my feet move in dance
Because you've made my soul light and free
Forever I will praise you and throughout eternity;
Always will I love you and bow my knees in prayer
As my heart longs for forever
And to meet you in the air…

Experiencing Jesus

Hearing His voice
Feeling His presence
Lets me know we are special and loved
Helps us to be able to carry on
When we have done the best we can

Hearing His voice
Feeling His presence
Makes the biggest problems not look so big
Makes all the worldly running to and fro
Seem to have no reason

Hearing His voice
Feeling His presence
Makes the things we stress over not so important
While giving peace and contentment beyond measure

Hearing His voice
Feeling His presence
Makes us truly love each other
And makes one long to hear and feel Him again.

In the Midst

Be in the midst of my heart, oh Lord
And speak: peace be unto you,
Breathe on me your Holy Spirit
As I continue this work with you,
For I am weak and lowly, oh Lord
And you are my strength,
Be in the midst of my heart, oh Lord
And never ever leave,

Be in the midst of my heart, oh Lord
As I prepare these simple words,
And hope a tiny seed of faith will drop
And You will be heard,
Be in the midst of my heart, oh Lord For I believe in You

The Dearest Friend I Have Ever Known

A true friend is one who loves you just the way you are, and not only sees who you are, but who you can become.

A true friend is there to share your everyday experiences and to catch you when you fall. A true friend accepts your worst, but helps you become your best.

This person understands your past and believes in your future. Then accepts you today just the way you are.

A true friend is one who comes in when the whole world has gone out.

True friendships are very valuable to us. We must nurture them. We must be able to cry together and laugh together. True friends lift us up and make us smile.

There is a friend that stands closer than a brother, who teaches us how to be a friend. When the whole world walks out on us, it is then when he walks in. That friend is Jesus.

What a friend we have in Jesus

You may think you're alone. You may even feel you're alone.
But Jesus says, you will never be alone, for I am with you.

The Child of God

It's a five-letter word and begins with a G.
That brings us through the most difficult times
Because of it we have made it through life thus far
It is how we have gotten through all the hardships
Through the valleys, over the mountains and through the storms.
When we hurt so badly from the loss of our loved ones, it is by this
that we make it though
The word is Grace, Grace, God's Grace
It is by His Grace that we make it through
Grace makes all the difference in our lives
We are at home in His Grace and love
His Grace is glorious and wonderful
God's Grace is manifold, all sufficient and all abundant
Hope, faith, forgiveness and salvation comes by the Grace of God
We are quickened by Grace
We are called by His Grace
We are saved by Grace through faith
Oh, sinner want you please
Come to Jesus and experience His saving Grace…

Amazing grace, how sweet the sound that
saved a wretch like me, I once was lost, but now
am found. T'was blind but now I see. T'was
Grace that taught my heart to fear and Grace, my
fears relieved, how precious did that grace appear,
the hour I first believed…(excerpt)

This is the Way

If a time should come along when you find yourself not knowing how to be strong and carry on, remember God.

During this time, it could make you feel like a deer caught in head lights, not being able to move an inch in any direction.

You know you're a Christian and have a personal relationship with Jesus Christ. You have felt his Holy Spirt many times. You read your Bible and pray every day. But now you find that you can't even think about what is right or wrong?

This thing has hit you full force, right in the face. You have never experienced anything like it before and don't know what to do.

Don't get lost in it and don't give up. Continue doing what's right. Keep walking one step at a time. Keep breathing one breath at a time. Stay in church and continue reading your Bible. Remain faithful, even though you feel completely alone.

Then when you are in the mist of the very hardest part, with your hands shaking, Jesus will show up. He will reach from behind and around you, then place his hands on your arms and help you travel on down the road. This is physically and spiritually real. He will hold you and guide you through this breathtaking time.

Jesus could be helping you understand a situation that you have seen someone go through and questioned him about, because you just didn't understand how a Christian could do something like that.

Or he could be letting you experience this to help someone who is struggling down the road, not knowing what to do.

Then again, he may just want you to be closer to him, to depend upon him and experience him in a greater way because he said that he would never leave you nor forsake you.

Yet, it could be for all these reasons because when God does something, it helps more than one person. It helps many people in many different ways.

Let Him help you.

♥

Comfort and Joy

Lord, you see and smell
Speak and hear
Touch and feel
You skip upon the hills…

What a difference your voice makes,
Your voice brings comfort,
When you speak the birds hush their singing,

What a difference your touch makes,
Your touch brings joy,
There is not another feeling like it in the world,

What a difference your presence makes.
Your presence brings comfort and joy

Sometimes you come
Just to be with us,
To sit and feel our heart
To be near us.

Sometimes you snuggle up
Next to us,
While making all the cares
Of this life disappear.

Being in your midst
Comforts us
And mends our broken heart

It is enough
Just being with You...

He Knows

As I live this life, walk this land, meet people of every kind
There is one that holds my hand and helps along the way
He guides through the wilderness and leads by the
waters where His milk and honey flows
He loves on me when I'm about to face a storm
And that love carries me through without any harm
Oh, I want to see Him
The one whom I have experienced through the years
And knows my every tear
The one who has protected and touched my heart
Whose voice gives me quite the start
Then shares a glimpse or two, that I can hardly contain
Oh, praise His holy name
Oh, I want to see Him
The one who knows what we need before we ask
The one who saved and gave me new life
My Savior, My Friend
Jesus

Master, Savior, Lord of All

No matter what comes my way
No matter what problems arise
As long as I am with you, I will survive;
When the storm clouds rise
When the hurt in my heart makes me cry
As long as you are with me, I will abide;
When it feels like my feet
Have been kicked out from under me
And it's all I can do to stand
As long as I can see your hand at work
I will understand;
Keep me near you, is my cry
Let me feel your presence;
Oh, Master, Savior, Lord of All
Forever be, not far from me…

Open my spiritual eyes that I may see Your perfect works.

Believe

You are in a bad place in your life
Your mind is dark as night,
You have been broken so badly that you can't seem to mend
Don't give up and don't give in
Someone is praying for you…
Everyone has left you and gone their own way
Now your alone and don't know how to pray
Someone is standing in the gap for you…
You need more to heal than anyone can give
And you've come to end of your way,
Just know someone's heart is breaking for you
Fall on your knees today…
Just fall on your knees and ask Jesus to
please forgive you of all your sins
Come into your heart and give you a new start
For with Jesus it all begins
Talk to Jesus today…

Learn of me.
Jesus

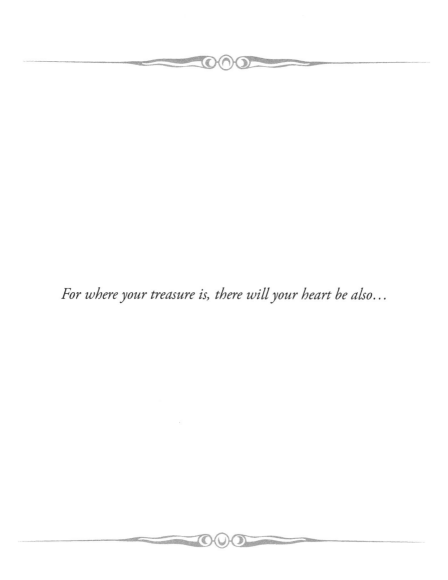

For where your treasure is, there will your heart be also...

About the Author

Donna Christopher grew up in a small town in Newnan, Georgia, with her loving mother teaching her about Jesus. She was a shy, sweet, girl who loved the Lord. But it wasn't until the age of eighteen that she accepted the Lord as her personal savior. Now, as a wife, mother of two sons, grandchildren and a full-time job at a bank, she has been blessed throughout the years. Since she has been saved. the Lord has blessed her by giving her spiritual stories that she has been able to bless others with. Now, she wants to bless others with her stories of faith and love that she has for the Lord. As you read these stories, Donna prays you are blessed.

Pam Pilcher

CPSIA information can be obtained
at www.ICGtesting.com
Printed in the USA
JSHW042235131020
8627JS00004BA/46

9 781644 684788